ASHFORD
THEN & NOW
REVISITED
IN COLOUR

STEVE R. SALTER

The
History
Press

For James.
For Mum and Dad.

In memory of
Bernard Royston Button 1928–2011
A true gentleman and character with an infectious enthusiasm for Old Ashford

Title page photograph: Upper High Street, 1965. One of the earliest discovered colour transparencies of the town in 1965 taken by local photographer Leslie Lindfield, this splendid view depicts the town as it looked in the swinging sixties, where independent traders are seen dominating the High Street. Many argue that this should still be the case today. *(Roger Lindfield)*

First published in 2012

The History Press
The Mill, Brimscombe Port
Stroud, Gloucestershire, GL5 2QG
www.thehistorypress.co.uk

British Library Cataloguing in Publication Data.
A catalogue record for this book is available from the British Library.

ISBN 978 0 7524 6627 9

Typesetting and origination by The History Press
Printed in India
Manufacturing managed by Jellyfish Print Solutions Ltd

CONTENTS

INTRODUCTION

O ver the years, Ashford has been subject to numerous changes to its character and historic fabric, changes that make the town what it is today. Many locals still argue over favoured periods in the town's sometimes colourful history and many prefer 'their' generation – for example the 1960s. Ashford as a once 'quaint' and 'sleepy' market town has changed as a 'town' more than most in its immediate vicinity, and one wonders why it was targeted by scores of sometimes unsympathetic redevelopment, leaving us all with distant memories. Was it because it starts with the letter 'A', someone asked me once? For me, to be truthful, I don't really think that was the reason, but it is certainly possible. The Buchanan Report of 1967 indicated that big things were going to happen to our town and that they certainly did.

After all these years, many still ask the question 'why?' And still nobody can give a genuine reason. For example; Why knock down Mummery's cottage? Why knock down the Saracen's Head Hotel? Why knock down the Lord Roberts public house in North Street

High Street (Middle) junction with North Street, 1968. This, the second Sainsbury's store in Ashford, not only showed the chain's commitment to the town but also the advent of self-service shopping. Today the former supermarket is home to Boots the Chemist which opened on the site in September 1979. *(Steve Salter Archive)*

Wolseley Road junction with Stone Street, 1974. A rare view showing the once commercial and residential north-east sector of the town which was severed upon the opening of the adjacent stage of the infamous Ringway in November 1974. *(Steve Salter Archive)*

when it was reputed to be the oldest building and hostelry in the town? It appears that no-one and no law stood in the planners' way when it came to pulling our lovely old market town apart. Since writing the 'Remember When' and 'Express Cuttings' pages for the *Kentish Express* I have been lucky enough to receive regular material from my loyal readers, for which I am grateful. As well as many letters and requests, which I always endeavour to answer, I receive negatives, slides, photographs and old newspapers, all of which show an event, a place or a street and I am always enlightened by changes, especially when it's a picture I haven't seen before. More often than not though, the enlightenment is tinged with sadness. So many gems were lost, but it would be unfair to point the finger at one person for these changes.

A different stance was taken by our predecessors in past times and there was certainly no duty of care to the town and its heritage which is a terrible shame but we must enjoy the remaining rich history that the town has to offer. Everywhere we look there is still a reminder of bygone Ashford. Many of these reminders entice conversation and memories from individuals who have originated from the town. Although there is currently an economic downturn, we Ashfordians remain poised for the future plans for Ashford, some of which have already been funded, so we shall see. The plans are said to further enhance the character of the Old Town, and hopefully they'll do just that. We certainly can't help being cautious.

This long-awaited sixth volume of photographs is guaranteed to interest those who are passionate about their ever-evolving town and remember the distant days of Ashford as it used to be. *Ashford Then & Now Revisited* follows on from *Remembering Ashford* and my previous works and contains previously unseen comparative local images spanning the last fifty years. For many of the images, this will be the first time they have been seen: for others the first time for many years. *Ashford Then & Now Revisited* continues a fascinating look at old Ashford the way things were, but here we also see how things appear today, and so get an idea of just how much things have actually changed.

Steve R. Salter, 2012

1

MARKET TOWN
OBSCURITIES

GASWORKS LANE JUNCTION with Godinton Road, 1969. This extremely rare photograph, taken from approximately outside the former Elephant and Castle public house, shows one of the early offices of the once-popular *Ashford Advertiser* newspaper which was established the same year by local journalist Rod Craig. The ground-breaking local publication ran until 1984 when the KM Group bought the independent title and renamed it the *Ashford Extra* which still excels today. Popular fish and chip takeaway Wye Fisheries is just out of view to the left of the picture.
(Bill and Martin Waters)

GASWORKS LANE JUNCTION with Godinton Road, 2011. Today there is barely a trace of the former newspaper offices and adjacent dwellings, both having been demolished many years ago. The adjacent former Ashford Market site is earmarked for redevelopment, and currently sits overgrown and unkempt partly owing to the economic downturn. *(Steve Salter)*

ELWICK ROAD, 1969. A splendid and forgotten view showing the top of Elwick Road near to where it joins the foot of Bank Street with the original Ashford cattle market entrance (pictured centre). This somewhat sentimental view shows just how busy the town used to be prior to the removal of the ancient market to Sevington in 1993, which in the opinion of some was a big mistake. The extensive site was first altered just under a year after this view was taken for the first stage of the construction of the Ringway, but owners Hobbs Parker eventually parted company with the site after it was again made smaller for the new High Speed 1 line.

(Bill and Martin Waters)

ELWICK ROAD, 2011. Many of the trees have gone together with the former market site and entrance in what is today known as Ashford's 20mph Shared Space scheme which was completed almost two years ago. Previously on a section of the original Ringway, traffic was converted to two-way and designs similar to those used in Holland were adapted to make this area more pleasant and above all safer, but not before the BBC's *Top Gear* presenter Jeremy Clarkson had something to say about the scheme. *(Steve Salter)*

ELWICK ROAD, 1969. Another view taken further to the right showing the old market and the house next door, which was once thought to have been the home of Gerald Brown, the greengrocer who traded from New Rents in the 1970s and '80s. The corner of established automotive trader and repairer Stanhay can be seen just creeping into view on the right. *(Bill and Martin Waters)*

ELWICK ROAD, 2011. Many of the trees in the old view were felled or diseased, but this view shows the local authority's efforts to replace them and recreate the charming atmosphere once fostered in this popular part of town where many attractive villas still stand. These were once used by the Ashford Urban District Council and its rural councils in the days prior to the town becoming a borough and the advent of a new Civic Centre.
(Steve Salter)

NEW STREET JUNCTION with Magazine Road, 1960. A superb view showing some of the many dwellings that disappeared during the early 1970s, this time for the installation of a new roundabout. This would have been the main approach for drivers entering the town from the A20, a part of New Street that once boasted at least five hostelries in a very short distance from each other, with the Prince Albert and the Prince of Orange (on the right) actually next door to one another. During the early 1970s, my pram made regular trips past these houses which were only a stone's throw away from my home. *(Bill and Martin Waters)*

NEW STREET ROUNDABOUT, 2011. The old houses disappeared in 1973 when the new roundabout was installed in the County Council's bid to remove two dangerous junctions at both Magazine Road and Western Avenue. The building on the left is today the premises of the reputable business of David Easton who has been repairing televisions and installing aerials for over forty years in the town, and is probably one of Ashford's longest-serving independents. He had previously been located in Hempsted Street. *(Steve Salter)*

NEW STREET, 1960. Upon finding this photograph, I was very happy as this is an extremely rare view showing New Street as it looked up until about 1970. The former premises of Jan Adam the photographer at no. 31 can be seen in the part weather-boarded building on the right with the premises of Edward 'Skip' Hudson's Tool Shop and Cycle Agent at nos 27–9 with Aubrey Gray's School of Motoring next door. *(Bill and Martin Waters)*

NEW STREET, 2011. What a difference fifty years makes. Barely anything survived in this section of New Street with the advent of new road construction, in particular the widening of the street outside Caffyns Garage during the early 1970s and of course the infamous Ringway. We can, though, still identify a few of the surviving buildings including the former premises of F. Knock and Co., the builder at nos 22–3 New Street, now the home of Swinton Insurance incorporating Peter S. Roberts. *(Steve Salter)*

NEW STREET, 1960. The old pictures get better and better with this splendid view showing the former Prince Albert public house at no. 109 New Street with the memorable and popular premises of J. Longley the grocer a few doors down at nos 97–9. Note the old-fashioned concrete lampposts and telegraph pole with insulators in this view which are rarely seen around the town today, although one still exists at the former railway works entrance.
(*Bill and Martin Waters*)

NEW STREET, 2011. Today the once-popular Prince Albert public house stands derelict awaiting its fate. There was an unsuccessful attempt to revive the hostelry by joining it with the former Prince of Orange into one pub, which was against the wishes of many of Ashford's traditional pub-lovers. Many have fond memories of the former Prince of Orange, which was also known as the 'Three Ones' – due to the fact that it is at no. 111 New Street. The premises of Longley and its adjacent dwellings disappeared in 1973 to widen the road. *(Steve Salter)*

ST GEORGES SQUARE, 1959. This absolute gem taken on early Kodak transparency film shows the tank in St Georges Square which was presented to Ashford on 1 August 1919 in recognition of the town's efforts during the war years. This hugely classic view shows the former Folkestone Glass Works on the right of the picture in the former premises of Ashford Cleaners who once occupied the site. Note the splendid selection of automotive history.
(Leslie and Roger Lindfield)

ST GEORGES SQUARE, 2011. Today the ageing tank has been repainted in its original livery and has a much-needed protective canopy which was built in 1988. The glassworks finally disappeared in 1985 when it was demolished for the Park Mall development. (*Steve Salter*)

STATION ROAD, 1969.
This colour view from
the end of the 1960s
shows the extensive
site of Crouch's Garage
sandwiched between the
former Ashford Working
Men's Club and the large
house named 'Fairlawn',
which once housed the
office of the Ministry
of Labour and National
Service and a private
dwelling. Many years
before though, it was
owned by the Working
Men's Club. Note the
presence of National
Benzole fuel, certainly a
name from the past.
(Bill and Martin Waters)

STATION ROAD, 2011. The extensive garage site was demolished in 2006 after standing derelict for several years, together with the office block. The old house at the corner of Dover Place disappeared many years back. Happily the former Working Men's Club has survived the bulldozer and today it is the newly opened Everest Inn Restaurant which is reputed to sell the finest Nepalese and Indian cuisine in Ashford, although the author has yet to try it! (*Steve Salter*)

STATION ROAD JUNCTION with Vicarage Lane, 1964. Difficult to picture today, this view shows the former garages of the East Kent Road Car Company which at the time were shared with Maidstone and District. Many locals will remember the row of houses in the distance and the detached houses pictured centre, one of which was owned by the late Philip Dormer, chiropodist, who was an acknowledged expert on the history of Eastwell Park. Many will remember the adjacent houses pictured to the right of the garage which were known as Quebec, Ontario and Alberta, and once stood opposite the junction of Vicarage Lane. *(Bryan Sales)*

STATION ROAD JUNCTION with Vicarage Lane, 2011. Both the older houses and business premises either side of the bus depot were demolished between 1966 and 1973, but the transport hub latterly owned by Stagecoach buses was demolished in 1999 to be replaced by Ashford Bowling. In recent years both Kanthack House and Greencoat House have undergone extensive refurbishment, the latter being converted into self-contained flats on the upper floor, with shop units below.
(Steve Salter)

2

TURN BACK TIME

BANK STREET, 1964. Taken for traffic survey purposes, this evocative view takes a look back at Bank Street at a time when pedestrianisation wasn't even thought of and traffic was actually two-way. The junction of Tufton Street can be seen on the right of the picture which at the time led to Hempsted Street and Regents Place among other nearby streets.
(Bryan Sales)

BANK STREET, 2011. The streaming traffic has been replaced by a manned gatehouse, thus during office hours only allowing vehicles by permit. The introduction of trees and continental-style seating is something of a trend in the town nowadays with almost every café allowing you to eat and drink in the street. Note how the new County Square extension in the distance looks inferior against the street's traditional buildings.
(Steve Salter)

BANK STREET, 1964. This time we take a look north towards the High Street and at some of the once-familiar names around at the time. Many locals will remember Nicholas Kingsman the baker on the left at the corner of Tufton Street, which had for many years previously been the home of a Lipton's store. We can also see Multi-Broadcast TV Rentals at no. 14 with the formidable Gizzi's Restaurant next door at no. 12. The popular restaurant run by the much-respected Vilma and Antonio Gizzi was one of two restaurants they ran in the town, and is said to have had the first jukebox situated in a café. The meeting point was listed in the *Day by Day* directory for Ashford as early as 1959. *(Bryan Sales)*

BANK STREET, 2011. Sadly these familiar haunts are no longer in the town and with such a wide range of places to choose from, it is sometimes difficult to create an atmosphere like before. The trees obscure this part of Bank Street today but it is still used as a main artery for buses and pedestrians into the town. Although this top section is largely dominated by solicitors such as Girlings, Kingsfords and Hallett and Co., the street contains many independent traders too, such as Green's Shoe Repairs (seen on the left), in what was once the bakery. It's a joy to still find such a traditional trade complete with after-sales service.
(Steve Salter)

LOWER HIGH STREET, 1962. If anyone, including newcomers to the town or the younger generation, wondered what Ashford was like in days gone by, then this picture illustrates it perfectly. With *Man's Favourite Sport?* starring Rock Hudson showing at the Odeon and cars parked at such odd angles outside, one can see just how different the town is today. Many of the buildings in the distance made way for redevelopment during the 1960s, including the premises of Alfred Olby, builders' merchant (pictured above the single-decker bus). This is a splendid picture showing our old market town at its very best. *(Bryan Sales)*

LOWER HIGH STREET, 2011. Almost an impossible task to recreate the previous view, this picture has been taken from an unlocked dormer window at no. 54 High Street and from a higher position, but shows how different the now-pedestrianised area looks today. Although not as large-scale, a selection of market stalls still gather in this area, where sheep and cattle were driven along generations before, an uneasy task perfectly depicted in the local famous painting by George Shepherd. One can't imagine what such a task would be like today.
(Steve Salter)

CASTLE STREET, 1962. This splendid view takes a rare look at some of the long-lost business premises of trader Knowles and Co., which operated in the town for a number of years and sold everything from furniture to televisions. Their premises pictured here at nos 6a, 8 and 10 Castle Street was opposite their main store at no. 7, and barely round the corner from their main furniture department at no. 106 High Street. The buildings illustrated had been bulldozed by 1974 when Park Street was widened, but the firm carried on business until the early 1980s. On closer inspection there is an AA sign telling motorists that North Street is blocked; isn't the No Entry sign enough!? (*Bryan Sales*)

CASTLE STREET, 2011. A service road for the rear of High Street premises has been created where Knowles once stood, and part of the Park Mall development (namely the Kall-Kwik store) stands on the junction where Park Street and Castle Street once met. It is sad to think that the original buildings (seen below) were sacrificed to be replaced by this ugly flank wall, and more to the point how planners got away with it. Thankfully the harsh attitude has disappeared today in favour of heritage and conservation. *(Steve Salter)*

CASTLE STREET, 1962. A fascinating view of Castle Street looking towards its junction with the High Street and New Rents. We can see the former Gutteridges Chemist pictured in the background at no. 107 High Street and butcher Charles Warner next door at no. 109, both of which disappeared in the early 1970s. The greatly missed restaurant and snack bar of Crameri's can be seen adjacent to the chemist on the left with Broome's the Tobacconists next door at no. 4 Castle Street. The memorable Goddard's Butchers at no. 1 New Street can be seen just creeping into view on the right, and was for many years run by kindly gentleman Tony Ansell. *(Bryan Sales)*

CASTLE STREET, 2011. There is barely a soul in sight in this view taken on a weekday in 2011. The Hospice Shop now occupies both nos 4 and 6 with the unusually named 'KOKO 4 Men' barbers occupying no. 2, which had at one time been the snack bar of Crameri's Restaurant. The former butchers premises of Goddard's on the right is currently vacant but has in recent times been a shop selling mobility scooters. *(Steve Salter)*

NEW STREET, 1960. Before acquiring this picture a couple of months back, I couldn't imagine that an image this rare could still exist. This view illustrates the former premises of Dray & Son, boot and shoemaker and also repairer at no. 24 New Street, which once stood near to Hayward's Garage, and the one time hostelry the New Inn which was bombed during the Second World War. The ramshackle building illustrated didn't survive for much longer after this picture was taken, and initially made way for an extension to the garage site. Today any trace would be buried under the Ringway. *(Bill and Martin Waters)*

NEW STREET, 2011. This key junction of the Ringway is approximately where the premises of Dray & Son once stood. Give that this is such a developed and altered area today, it would be impossible to pinpoint its whereabouts exactly. The Park Mall Shopping Centre can be seen in the background. *(Steve Salter)*

HEMPSTED STREET looking towards New Rents, 1960. In answer to many requests, as promised another rare view of Hempsted Street before it was totally obliterated in the name of progress. This vastly characterful street is still spoken of fondly today and many locals were either raised or knew someone in the street before it was swept away for the Tufton Shopping Centre development. The street boasted three hostelries, namely the Coach and Horses (pictured left), the Wellington Hotel (in the foreground) and the Invicta at the corner of Hempsted Street and Godinton Road – a sad reminder of what planners were once capable of.
(Bill and Martin Waters)

COUNTY SQUARE NCP car park, 2011. This is sadly what ended up replacing Hempsted Street. Although there are shopping malls above, this is approximately where the earlier picture would have been taken. Our planning predecessors have been named and shamed before, but this is a prime example of 1970s ruthlessness.
(Steve Salter)

REGENTS PLACE, 1961. In an attempt to always give readers something different, this rarity shows Regents Place before the construction of the town's telephone exchange, which was completed in 1964. The earmarked site, which at one time housed a windmill, was adjacent to New Rents and skirted by Prospect Place which consisted of twelve dwellings. The premises of Swinard's Tyre Service can be seen on the right with Forge Lane in the background. *(Roger Jones)*

REGENTS PLACE, 2011. Looking vastly different today, the telephone exchange makes this area to many, totally unrecognisable. Many of the terraces in the previous view to the immediate left were replaced in the 1980s by more modern equivalents but at least those further along can still be picked out from these comparative views. *(Steve Salter)*

BANK STREET, 1970. In the days before the opening of the Ringway, traffic still crawled through the town's narrow and sometimes overcrowded streets, but this pre-Ringway shot shows a rather deserted view of Bank Street, somewhat different from those seen earlier in the book. Commercial Union House (latterly Trafalgar House) can be seen on the right of the picture together with the handsome estate agency premises of Burrows and Co. at nos 39–41 Bank Street, also on the right. The former Market Hotel is just out of view on the left at the corner of Godinton Road.
(David Worsley/Studio Photocraft)

BANK STREET, 2011. The somewhat imposing extension of County Square certainly dominates the left of the picture, with Trafalgar House on the right, nowadays complete with shop units under its offices. The former estate agents' premises is today the popular bar and restaurant Utopia, the building having been largely rebuilt and refurbished after Burrows' departure. *(Steve Salter)*

3

FORGIVE
AND NOT FORGET

GODINTON ROAD, 1961. An atmospheric view of how things looked in Godinton Road back at the start of the 1960s and before any destruction took place. Here we can see scores of terraces with small business premises sandwiched between in this nostalgic photograph showing this end of Godinton Road in its entirety. Its junction with Bank Street can be seen in the distance with the former Elephant and Castle public house and the junction of Apsley Street on the immediate left. Just out of view, the popular fish and chip takeaway Wye Fisheries once traded from premises near to the junction of Gasworks Lane. *(Roger Jones)*

GODINTON ROAD, 2011. Until 2006, you were still able to get an unobstructed view from this point looking along Godinton Road towards Bank Street, but today the County Square extension makes that impossible. Despite efforts to let them, these huge units illustrated have been vacant since the completion of the works in 2008. Today the former 'Elephant' is known as the Oranges and still proves popular on the drinking and social circuit in the town.
(Steve Salter)

GODINTON ROAD, 1961. This superb view shows Godinton Road looking towards its junction with Bank Street through to Queen Street, and we see the once-popular Maylam's Restaurant on the left at the corner of Hempsted Street. Many will remember the premises of C. Knight the greengrocer at no. 5 on the right and at one time the newsagents business of Mrs E.A. Reed next door at no. 7. The premises directly adjacent to the lamppost on the right were called 'Hemsted Terrace' – a slightly different spelling to the street it once faced.
(Roger Jones)

COUNTY SQUARE, LOWER OVAL, 2011. Today the lower floor of the recently completed County Square extension covers this part of Godinton Road, which was still a through-road and open-air car park in 2005. The automatic doors pictured in the distance look towards Queen Street. Hempsted Street would have been to the immediate left. *(Steve Salter)*

HEMPSTED STREET, 1961. This gem of a photograph gives a fantastic view of Hempsted Street from its junction with Godinton Road and shows both junctions with Middle Street and Tufton Street further along on the right. Although there was a mismatch of building styles in the street, in my opinion each of them had their merit both visually and historically – in particular those seen in the distance (centre). *(Roger Jones)*

COUNTY SQUARE, LOWER OVAL, 2011. Again tarmac and dwellings have gone in favour of concrete and shops in this view taken from the Lower Oval in the County Square extension, showing approximately where the lower part of Hempsted Street once stood.
(Steve Salter)

GODINTON ROAD, 1961. A splendid view showing the much-loved and greatly missed Invicta public house at the corner of Hempsted Street, a stone's throw away from the Elephant and Castle which can just be seen further along on the right at the foot of Apsley Street. At one time, one of the dwellings pictured adjacent to the Invicta was the home of C. Rolfe the turf accountant, although all appear to be houses in this view. *(Roger Jones)*

COUNTY SQUARE, GODINTON ROAD ENTRANCE, 2011. Children's store Kid's Stuff and clothing retailer New Look occupy the spot where the Invicta and adjacent terraces once stood. Prior to the construction of this extension archaeologists were called in to the site to ascertain any possible important ancient history on the site. *(Steve Salter)*

CHURCH ROAD, 1970. This excellent view shows the Congregational church which stood at the corner of Church Road and Tufton Street and this is one of the clearest and most unobstructed views that has been published for a long time. The old premises of J.W. Hall can be seen on the right near the trees, with the town's current police station completed in 1969 just creeping into view on the left. The handsome ecclesiastical landmark was demolished in 1972 to be replaced by a somewhat one-dimensional and ugly Magistrates Court building. *(David Worsley/Studio Photocraft)*

CHURCH ROAD, 2011. While dodging the action in a bowls match, I took this view at the edge of the green, and realised just how much is obscured by trees in the summer months. The police station can be clearly seen just after the second tree from the left, but the modernist Court Buildings are adequately hidden from view – besides, one would much rather see a church with its spire than a court building. *(Steve Salter)*

ELWICK ROAD, 1969. A fascinating view showing Elwick Road in the days before the Ringway construction and any Shared Space scheme was thought of – or a 20mph speed limit for that matter. The curve in the road disappeared two years later when part of the cattle market site was purchased for phase 1 of the Ringway, which ran parallel with Godinton Road and joined up with West Street. Note the great selection of old-fashioned cars in this view.
(David Worsley/Studio Photocraft)

ELWICK ROAD, 2011. The recently completed Shared Space scheme has redefined the once-bustling road which was something of a racetrack before the alterations took place. While retaining its historic villas at this point, Elwick Road is further complimented by continental-style surfaces and modern street-lighting design.
(Steve Salter)

NORTH STREET, 1970. Back in the days before redevelopment, North Street was still a through-road and a main route into the heart of the town. Shortly before any alterations took place, this is how it looked. The premises of John Hogbin the estate agent (seen on the left), together with the Lord Roberts public house (on the right), were sacrificed for a service road and subsequent widening of Park Street upon the construction of Charter House. The doctor's house of Drs Don and Elliott has gone at this time – it had stood at the point of the gap further down on the left-hand side of the road. (*David Worsley/Studio Photocraft*)

NORTH STREET, 2011. Despite plans to totally destroy North Street, which were proposed in 1962, today's planners and authorities have taken the conscientious decision to protect the remainder of North Street by making it a Conservation Area, a stance that should have been taken years ago. While Hogbin's premises wasn't of any particular architectural merit, the former Lord Roberts hostelry was deemed to be one of the oldest buildings and certainly the oldest inn in the town at the time of its demolition in 1972. As illustrated, North Street is no longer a through-road and it has been tastefully paved with both brick paving and granite setts for the road surface. (*Steve Salter*)

NORTH STREET, 1970. This view shows the opposite side of North Street with the Lord Roberts pub just creeping into view on the right. The junction of Park Street can be seen on the left. The one-time furnisher W.H. Gibbs' premises can be seen on the right at no. 14, and they also had premises adjacent to Lewis and Hyland's menswear department at nos 97–9 High Street. (David Worsley/Studio Photocraft)

NORTH STREET, 2011. Today North Street is somewhat protected from the Ringway by the offices of the Kentish Express and RBS pictured in the distance, and it would be fair to say that the remainder of the ancient thoroughfare is one of the most attractive areas in the heart of central Ashford. Pizza Express now operates their successful restaurant chain from the former premises of W.H. Gibbs. (Steve Salter)

CHURCH ROAD, 1973. A post-Congregational church view of the top of Church Road at its junction with Tufton Street and Vicarage Lane. Here we see Tufton House, which was at one time home of the Employment Tribunal Service, and which replaced the former premises of J.W. Hall who had moved to Cobbs Wood by this time. The fenced-off area on the left where the church once stood has been converted into a temporary car park at this point. The attractive white-fronted Clergy House can be seen in the background. *(David Worsley/ Studio Photocraft)*

CHURCH ROAD, 2011. Parked cars still dominate the junction of Church Road with Vicarage Lane thirty-eight years later. The Magistrates Court (to the left of the picture) is a rather crude replacement for the once-charming church which was dismantled in 1972. One reader of my weekly *Kentish Express* column informs me that she still has one of the doors to the former church as the door to her house, and rather solidly built it is too! *(Steve Salter)*

4

BACK IN THE DAY

APSLEY STREET, 1961. Many local residents still refer to the terraced dwellings of Apsley Street, which are illustrated here being dismantled, stripped of their saleable fixtures and fittings like doors, floorboards and fireplaces. The dwellings which backed onto Hempsted Street were bulldozed to eventually be replaced by the Tufton Centre, but those on the left of the picture survive to this day. The rear of those premises in New Rents, which were also demolished for redevelopment, can be seen in the distance.
(Roger Jones)

APSLEY STREET, 2011. The town centre residential street, although used by service vehicles and shoppers using the two NCP car parks at the shopping centre, does have its quiet periods, as illustrated here. The street is one-way in the direction of New Rents, and as a location to set up residence, still proves popular despite being overlooked by commercial property.
(Steve Salter)

HIGH STREET JUNCTION with North Street, 1967. Another extremely rare view showing this key vacant site, previously occupied by the Saracen's Head Hotel, which had been cleared to commence construction of Ashford's first self-service Sainsbury's. The resulting iconic structure, built by local reputable builder Epps, was open for business by 1968 and stretched back to Park Street where the supermarket chain built their store which opened ten years later. Today Boots the Chemist occupies the imposing corner spot in the town centre.

(David Worsley/Studio Photocraft)

HIGH STREET JUNCTION with North Street, 2011. Today Boots still occupy the prime position on the High Street and have celebrated their 100th year in the town having opened their first store at nos 60–2 High Street in 1911. After a conversion from glass-fronted supermarket to chemist, this Boots store opened in September 1979.
(Steve Salter)

TUFTON STREET, 1971. A rare view showing the former almshouses in Tufton Street which were once situated behind the Wellington Hotel in Hempsted Street and opposite the Elwick Club and post office. In 1972 the area was compulsorily purchased for the Tufton Shopping Centre development and both the almshouses and Elwick Club together with the whole of Hempsted Street was cleared for the project. Brand new almshouses were built on church land opposite the bowling green in Vicarage Lane in 1973 and a new Elwick Club opened in Church Road the same year.
(Ken Foster/Burrows & Co.)

TUFTON STREET, 2011. Today the Tufton Street entrance to County Square (previously the Tufton Centre) together with stores such as Johnsons the Cleaners, are situated where the almshouses once stood, although you can pick out the window frontage and brickwork of today's Wimpy Bar which had previously been Flinns the cleaners.
(Steve Salter)

NORTH STREET, 1962. This photograph taken from the dormer window of what at the time would have been the Mocha Bar, gives a great insight into North Street as it looked in such a vastly different era. The Saracen's Head Hotel can be seen on the left of the picture just under two years before its demolition to make way for a new Sainsbury's, and the premises of John Collier, tailor, is on the right of the picture. It is said that customers of the Mocha Bar would regularly hold their breath as two double-decker buses passed each other at this tricky point in the High Street. Note the extent of the Saracen's Head building and the presence of traffic signals. *(Bryan Sales)*

NORTH STREET, 2011. This is the same view in 2011 which shows just how much closer the former hotel stood to the road, and just how much things have changed in the familiar town centre street. *(Steve Salter)*

UPPER HIGH STREET, 1964. This photograph, taken from the top of Bank Street where it meets High Street, gives a fascinating insight into the way things were in previous times. The premises of Montague Burton, tailors, can be seen at nos 74–6 High Street together with Timothy Whites, chemist, at nos 70–2 next door. The old Top Rank premises can be seen on the right in the one-time chambers of Ashford Urban District Council. *(Bryan Sales)*

UPPER HIGH STREET, 2011. The former premises of Timothy Whites, which latterly amalgamated with Boots, has disappeared in favour of a new store for WH Smith built in 1986, but Burton, as they are now known, still survives today on the same site. The former premises of Top Rank has in recent years become home of Ernest Jones, jeweller, with longstanding and respected hairdresser Christophe on the upper floor.
(Steve Salter)

NORTH STREET, 1962. An unusual view taken from the roof of the former Ashley Russell's store at no. 2 North Street, gives a clear and unobstructed view of the main artery into the town from the A28. The view also shows some of the traders that were in the town at the time, including Jacksons Hairdresser at no. 3a and Fendall's Wine, Spirit, Beer and Cyder Merchants at no. 9. The double-decker buses advertising the *Kent Messenger* newspaper were a familiar sight during the 1960s.

(Bryan Sales)

NORTH STREET, 2011. Taken from approximately the same spot, this modern view shows vast changes in North Street. The most noticeable being the lack of traffic and the presence of the Boots building which makes this and the earlier view totally recognisable to many. *(Steve Salter)*

ELWICK ROAD, 1963. A rare view showing the last few days of the Corn Exchange at the top of Elwick Road and the foot of Bank Street, and in particular the former premises of Ward & Humphries, china shop. They had vacated the Corn Exchange which was literally awaiting its fate, and was demolished shortly after this picture was taken. Many an event and gathering was held at the once-popular meeting point, but nevertheless in their wisdom the old Urban District Council granted permission for its destruction. What a valuable asset it would have been today. (*Bryan Sales*)

ELWICK ROAD, 2011. Initially the Corn Exchange was replaced by these offices which were for the Commercial Union Group, so the building was aptly named Commercial Union House and signage reflected that on this elevation at the time. The company had moved here from premises they had previously occupied at nos 89–91 High Street, which is today partly the upper floor of Starbucks. In the 1970s though, the CU moved out. By this time, the council were interested and the building was named Trafalgar House. They used it until the construction of the Civic Centre in 1983. *(Steve Salter)*

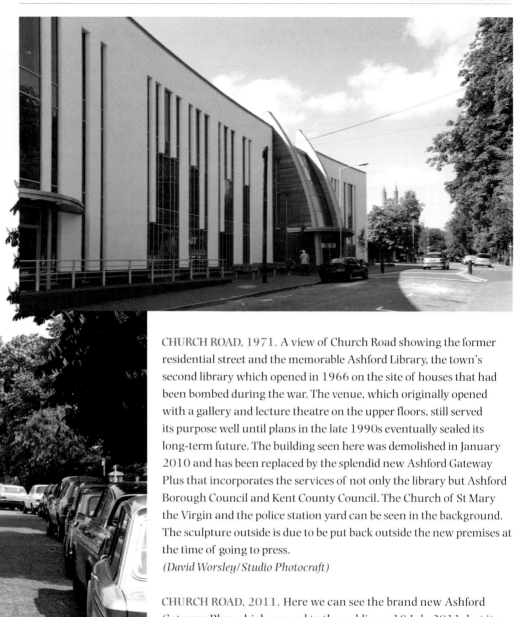

CHURCH ROAD, 1971. A view of Church Road showing the former residential street and the memorable Ashford Library, the town's second library which opened in 1966 on the site of houses that had been bombed during the war. The venue, which originally opened with a gallery and lecture theatre on the upper floors, still served its purpose well until plans in the late 1990s eventually sealed its long-term future. The building seen here was demolished in January 2010 and has been replaced by the splendid new Ashford Gateway Plus that incorporates the services of not only the library but Ashford Borough Council and Kent County Council. The Church of St Mary the Virgin and the police station yard can be seen in the background. The sculpture outside is due to be put back outside the new premises at the time of going to press.
(David Worsley/Studio Photocraft)

CHURCH ROAD, 2011. Here we can see the brand new Ashford Gateway Plus which opened to the public on 18 July 2011, but its official opening was in October 2011. The standard set for both facilities and construction is very high and one has to praise both the authorities and those who managed the project from the outset. It is a far cry from its predecessor which was only a quarter of its size. The new Gateway Plus is an asset to the town and also boasts a pleasant café on the second floor which is accessible to all.
(Steve Salter)

LOWER HIGH STREET, 1970. Back in the days before pedestrianisation, the Lower High Street was still a busy thoroughfare and by 1970, traffic was one-way in the direction of East Hill. The traffic flow changed considerably over the years, and schemes such as buses using the left-hand side and car parking in the centre of the road came and went, but the street was first partly pedestrianised in 1976, only to be fully pedestrianised by 1999. (David Worsley/Studio Photocraft)

LOWER HIGH STREET, 2011. It is difficult to achieve the same shot today due to the introduction of trees and street furniture, but this is how the once-busy road looks today. The creation of a fountain provides a pleasant focal point for the High Street which, at its widest point, is reputed to be one of the broadest in the country. (Steve Salter)

5

FORGOTTEN CORNERS

MAIDSTONE ROAD JUNCTION with Chart Road and Western Avenue, 1960. One of the earliest colour slides of the town, this very rare view shows the old triple junction of Chart Road where it joins Maidstone Road and Western Avenue. This key artery from the A28 to and from Tenterden and further afield was classed as an accident blackspot and by 1968, plans were afoot to rid the town of such danger. It wasn't until 1973 that the junction was altered and replaced as part of the nearby Ringway construction. The original Church of St Teresa of Avila can be seen in the background. *(Roger and Leslie Lindfield)*

MAIDSTONE ROAD, 2011. The dangerous accident blackspot is no more and today there is no trace of the former triple junction, but sadly the old Roman Catholic church has disappeared too, its destruction granted in 1993 to be replaced by the current church, which certainly hasn't got the character or the architectural merit of its predecessor. *(Steve Salter)*

MAIDSTONE ROAD, 1960. This view, again pretty obscure, shows an early colour shot of a wedding at the Church of St Teresa of Avila, with the old house next door, which was also demolished as part of the plans of the early 1990s. Note the statue of St Teresa (far right). The ornate statue still survives in the grounds of the new church today.
(Roger and Leslie Lindfield)

MAIDSTONE ROAD, 2011. Sadly nothing remains (apart from the aforementioned statue) of the old church which stood on the site, nor its surrounding buildings. With a growing congregation, it can be appreciated that a larger church was needed, but to demolish something of such heritage, character and architectural merit is beyond me. (*Steve Salter*)

NORWOOD STREET, 1966. Difficult to picture today, this is where the rear of the police station and entrance to the yard now stands in Norwood Street, but here we can see some of its buildings including the former Ebenezer Chapel (built 1863) being dismantled for the new local headquarters which opened in 1969. Further along on the right, F.C. Wood, funeral director, had premises too. *(Steve Salter Archive)*

NORWOOD STREET, 2011. This picture was taken in the same position as the 1966 photograph above, and shows the police station which opened in 1969 and the rear stairs to the Front Office. Up until 1987, my father was a traffic sergeant based in Ashford and I've lost count of how many times I went into the station as a young child.
(Steve Salter)

ST GEORGES SQUARE/NEW STREET, 1959. The tank in St Georges Square which was presented to the town on 1 August 1919 is seen here long before any protective cover was thought of. Its final resting place outside the Old Prince of Wales public house has over the years been a regular talking point and it has also appeared in a number of guises during this time. It is regularly maintained and it is now painted the right colour for its model and era. At one time local utility provider Seeboard were permitted to house a sub-station inside the tank's interior, although this was removed many years ago. *(Steve Salter Archive)*

ST GEORGES SQUARE, 2011.
The First World War tank as it
looks today with its protective
cover which was built in 1988.
Many will remember the former
New China City Restaurant
which used to stand behind
the landmark in the 1970s
and would feature in many
photographs taken of the tank.
(Steve Salter)

TUFTON CENTRE, 1979. Many people of my generation and older will remember the former open-air Tufton Centre with fondness and some of the stores that the centre has had to offer over the years. Here we see the one-time town centre supermarket of Tesco, which also had a home and wear department on the upper floor. The store opened in 1975, when the centre was brand new but closed on 1 August 1987 in favour of out-of-town shopping. Fosters Menswear can be seen to the far left. Many will remember the oast house-style kiosks (right) which sold everything from sweets to jewellery.
(Steve Salter Archive)

COUNTY SQUARE, 2011. The difference is certainly clear as in 1989 the Tufton Centre became County Square, and then owners CIN Properties invested millions to refurbish the town centre shopping experience and place a modern glass roof over the whole development. The former Tesco originally became Littlewoods but nowadays the two-storey unit is the home of BHS. The old kiosks were ditched in the new design in favour of a rather more open-plan feel. This is the Centre Square of the development.
(Steve Salter)

TUFTON CENTRE, 1979. Another view showing the former Tesco supermarket and the Marshallshop kiosk which sold sweets, drinks and newspapers back in the day. Many will remember the planted seating areas that the old centre had to offer.
(Steve Salter Archive)

COUNTY SQUARE,
2011. This view
shows the Centre
Square with its Costa
Coffee outlet.
(Steve Salter)

TUFTON STREET looking towards Hempsted Street, 1970. This view, one of my favourites of lost Ashford, shows a very rare depiction of Tufton Street looking through to Hempsted Street and the Coach and Horses public house in the distance, shortly before the advent of the new shopping centre. The former Elwick Club can be seen on the right next door to the post office, the latter still surviving today. Everything past the post office (pictured) was demolished for the project.
(*Steve Salter Archive*)

TUFTON STREET, 2011. What a vast difference forty years makes, but at least we can see that the post offfice is still going strong.
(Steve Salter)

UPPER HIGH STREET, 1970. Another of my personal favourites, this view shows the High Street shortly before the development that changed this scene forever. Everything was demolished from the tall building of Lewis and Hyland's menswear department, right along New Rents. This was for phases 1 and 2 of the Tufton Centre project. It's great to see such names as Hepworths (tailor), Clement Clarke (optician), and Brighter Homes (decorating specialists), on the left and Woolworths, Dolcis and International Stores on the right, as none of the traders exist today. *(Steve Salter Archive)*

UPPER HIGH STREET, 2011.
The busy road and traffic
lights have gone in favour of
a pleasant pedestrian-friendly
area complete with trees,
seating and a bandstand area.
It still seems really sad and
odd to note the absence of
Woolworths on the High Street.
(Steve Salter)

UPPER HIGH STREET. This view from winter 1976 shows the former International Stores on the left-hand side which eventually closed in 1980 after many years in the town. The supermarket was demolished in 1985 to create an entrance for the Park Mall Shopping Centre. The first phase of the Tufton Centre is complete and open for business at this time, but the hoarding on the right illustrates that phase 2 had yet to be completed. Eventually Marks & Spencer took a large percentage of the land, and opened a new store as part of the phase 2 development. *(Steve Salter Archive)*

UPPER HIGH STREET, 2011. Again pedestrianisation has proved the right decision on the High Street. *(Steve Salter)*

ACKNOWLEDGEMENTS

O ver the years many local people and companies have been extremely kind and patient in assisting me with my research. Many have given me very valuable information, which has enabled me to put together an interesting record of the history of Ashford and to build up a substantial photographic collection.

I am overwhelmed by the continued support for and huge success of *Changing Ashford*, *Ashford Then and Now*, *Ashford 1950–1980*, *Around Ashford* and *Remembering Ashford*. I am also very grateful to those who have followed my fortunes over the years. Without their kindness this book wouldn't be possible. As always, I have received much generosity from individuals and organisations that have readily allowed me to use their pictures. I would therefore like to give special thanks to the following: James Adams; Richard Filmer, Gould and Harrison Estate Agents; Sylvia and Sid Marsh; Peter and Pam Goodwin; David Worsley; Geoff Mathews; Sam Mathews; Dan Mathews; Paul Rawlings; Jim Ashby and Mrs Joan Ashby; Howard and Christine Green; Allan and Lynn Ward; June at Ashford Gateway Plus (Library); Alastair Irvine, Robert Barman, Thom Morris, James Scott, Dan Bloom, Gary Browne, Martin Apps, Sam Lennon, Barry Hollis and all at the Kent Messenger Group; John and Val Williams; Pam Herrapath and Ray Wilkinson at Ashford Borough Council; Betty Shadwell; Roger Lindfield; Roger Jones; Mark Smith; Teresa Reed; Melvin Bartholomew; Bryan Badham; Vivienne Kenny; Allen and Mrs Christine Wells; Palma and Frankie Laughton; Jo-an Baxter; Sue Gambrill; Helene Coetzee; Mr and Mrs Keith Brown; Rita Deverill; Jon Barrett; Terry and Christine Baker, Terry Baker Electrical Contractor Limited; Bob and Daphne Davidson; David Geoghegan; David and Jean Emmett; Paul Cook at Dukelease Properties; Owen Holmes; Beverley Walsh and Matt Taylor at Barclays Ashford; David Easton; Mary and Shaun Hadley; Maxine Curtis; Shaun Milburn; Lindsay and Lesley at Cross's Ashford; Richard Stafford; Andrew and staff at The Merchant Chandler; Waterstones Ashford; Tracey McKeen at Ashford Gateway Plus Tourist Information; John Kennedy, architect; Susy, Mandy and Pauline at KM reception; Terry and Eunice Burch; Katherine Burch; Terry Woodcock; Kevin Brown and all at Snappy Snaps; Valerie Epps, International House; Esmé Rand.

I would also like to express my gratitude to the regular readers and contributors of material for my *Kentish Express* 'Remember When' and 'Express Cuttings' page that I have been writing since April 2009. I would like to thank the paper's editor Robert Barman and the news editor Alastair Irvine for my weekly blank canvas and their continued faith in my work. I am indebted to Sylvia and Sid Marsh and also David Worsley for the fantastic negatives that they keep finding for me – you are all very kind.

I would finally like to express a special thanks to my friend James for taking me under his wing and looking after me through long illness and difficult times in particular with my Mum who has Vascular Dementia. Thanks are also due to anyone whose name has not been acknowledged here, either through an oversight or because the original source or present ownership of pictures is unknown or unavailable. Many thanks as ever to Michelle Tilling and Richard Leatherdale at the History Press for your continued support and above all patience.

Do you have any pictures, negatives or colour slides, from the past fifty years in particular, that you would be willing to share with readers of the *Kentish Express* 'Remember When' page?
If so, send them with brief details to Steve Salter, Kentish Express Remember When, 34–6 North Street, Ashford, Kent, TN24 8JR, or by e-mail to rememberwhen_kmash@hotmail.co.uk.
You can also contact Steve via the splendid Facebook group – Ashford: Remembering the Way it Once Was – where local residents and those passionate about the town can and do share their pictures and memories. The group, set up by local resident Mark Smith, has over 3,000 images and over 2,000 members, and is well worth a visit.